The Genesis of Genesis

"If There Had been no Sin, There would have been no Suffering"

by
Dan Obubeleye Pokima

DORRANCE
PUBLISHING CO
EST. 1920
PITTSBURGH, PENNSYLVANIA 15238

Dorrance Publishing Co
585 Alpha Drive
Pittsburgh, PA 15238
Visit our website at *www.dorrancebookstore.com*

ISBN: 979-8-8860-4437-9
eISBN: 979-8-8860-3858-9

Table of Contents

Acknowledgements

This book is dedicated to the faithful saints of God at the Institute for Creation Research (ICR) and the faithful friends of ICR who are no longer with us. They are, Dr. Henry M. Morris, an American engineer, a pioneer, and founder of ICR; Dr. Henry M. Morris III, a great visionary; Dr. Duane Gish, an American biochemist and a master debater; Dr. Bob Armstrong, a skilled orthopedic surgeon; Dr. John Whitcomb, an American theologian; and my former pastors: Pastor Emeritus of Calvary Baptist Church New York City; Dr. Stephen Olford, a trailblazer; Dr. Donald Hubbard, declared the whole counsel of God, and my Sunday School teacher, Mr. Jiles Brooks taught the Word of God with clarity. Like the Apostle Paul, every one of them could say, "I have fought a good fight, I have finished my course, I have kept the faith" (2 Timothy 4:7). And indeed, they did, and the Lord said to every one of them, "Well done, thou good and faithful servant" (Matthew 25:21). For over three decades, I have been a friend and a student of ICR, which is now based in Dallas, Texas.

My sincere thanks go to the faithful scientists and staff at ICR. I was introduced to ICR by my late spiritual parents, Paul and Caroline London, in New York City. ICR has made a profound influence in my life, in science and the scriptures, and in my daily walk with my Savior the Lord Jesus Christ. I know all that I know about ICR from a fifteen-minute radio program, "Science, Scripture, and Salvation, Days of Praise," a quarterly "Daily Bible Readings and Devotional Commentaries," and a monthly "Acts and Facts Magazine," and DVDs with state-of-the-art technology. ICR has well-qualified scientists known as "creationist scientists" in any discipline. ICR is not a local congregation, but its commitment to "Solo Scriptura" (the Scripture alone) far surpasses that of some local congregations.

I have watched, listened, and read articles by both creationists and evolutionists. I do not consider myself to be an authority or an expert, but I do consider myself to be enlightened and well-informed. The creation/evolution debate is, in a real sense, the most fundamental issue of all. As a student of ICR, I know that I stand on a solid and an unshakable ground because they have the mind of Christ. They are humble and faithful servants who give Christ the preeminence in all that they do, both in science and scripture. They are also theologians and see no conflict between science and the Scriptures. They wholly trust the inerrancy, infallibility, and sufficiency of the Scriptures. They boldly keep their conversation (manner of life), integrity, reputation, and research under the demands of the Scriptures. The Scriptures demand that, "In the beginning God created the heaven and the earth" (Genesis 1:1). The Creator and Savior is non-other than the Lord Jesus Christ. The Apostle Paul said, "I am set for the defence of the gospel" (Philippians 1:17). Like the Apostle Paul, every one of the saints at ICR and others that were acknowledged could also say, "I am set for the defence of the gospel." Listen to Job, "I have esteemed the words of his mouth more than my necessary food" (Job 23:12). Wow! I also believe that the staff at ICR and others will also concur with Job.

Soli Deo Gloria.

Introduction

Webster's Dictionary defines Genesis as, "A coming into being: ORIGIN." Cambridge English Dictionary defines Genesis as, "The time when something came into existence; the beginning or origin." Therefore, the universe we live in had a beginning, and every known problem or societal ill facing humanity today had a beginning, too! It was the result of Adam's transgression of the law of God "sin" in the Garden of Eden. These problems are primarily recorded in the First Book of the Bible, Genesis, and other books of the Bible in the New Testament. Is it a coincidence that the first book in the Bible is called Genesis? Adam and Eve were the first human beings.

According to the late evolutionary astronomer, cosmologist, and author Carl Sagan, "The Cosmos is all that is, or ever was, or ever will be." According to the two definitions above, the cosmos had a beginning. Therefore, the statement by Sagan is nothing but "vain imagination" (Romans 1:21), and it is contrary to Genesis 1:1, Psalm 33:6, 9, and Hebrews 11:3. And other passages of Scripture. You don't have to be a scientist to know that the cosmos is "a well-ordered whole." It is from the Greek kosmos which means "order and harmony." The Earth rotates or revolves around the sun and gives us day and night with precision. The distance between the sun and the earth is just the right distance. If it is just one degree more, we will all be burned up or a degree less and we will all freeze to death! "In the beginning, God created the heaven and the earth" (Genesis 1:1). "And God said, Let the earth bring forth grass, the herd yielding seed, and the fruit tree yielding fruit after his kind, whose seed is in itself, upon the earth and it was so. And the earth brought forth grass and herb yielding seed after his kind, and the tree yielding fruit, whose seed was in itself, after his kind: and God

vii

saw that it was good" (vv.11-12)."And God said, Let there be lights in the firmament of the heaven to divide the day from the night; and let them be for signs, and for seasons, and for days, and years….And God made two great lights: the greater light to rule the day, and the lesser light to rule the night: he also made the stars" (vv.14-16). "Those who scoff at the Bible, might think that this is like an afterthought. However, there is nothing like an afterthought with God." God admired His handywork and saw nothing but beauty. "And God saw everything that he had made, and, behold, it was very good. And the evening and the morning were the sixth day" (v.31). Six days of creation!

According to Sagan, the world has always existed "eternal." The Almighty God is the only Eternal Being, The Alpha and The Omega, The Beginning and The End of all things! Listen to this, "LORD, thou hast been our dwelling place in all generations. Before the mountains were brought forth, or ever thou hadst formed the earth and the world, even from everlasting to everlasting thou art God" (Psalm 90:1-2). Wow! According to the Holy Bible, the Word of God, the universe had a beginning and never was and will not ever be.

Pay attention to this; "But the day of the Lord will come as a thief in the night; in the which the heavens shall pass away with a great noise, and the elements shall melt with fervent heat, the earth also and the works that are therein shall be burned up. Seeing then that all these things shall be dissolved, what manner of persons ought ye to be in all holy conversation and godliness" (2 Peter 3:10-11). "In the beginning God created the heaven and the earth" (Genesis 1:1). "By the word of the LORD were the heavens made; and all the host of them by the breath of his mouth. For he spake, and it was done; he commanded, and it stood fast" (Psalm 33:6, 9, Psalm 102:25, Psalm 104:24-25, Proverbs 3:19, Nehemiah 9:6, Isaiah 42:5, 45:18, 48:13, Romans 1:20, Hebrews 11:3). God clearly manifested Himself to mankind in the above Scripture passages. These are all supernatural. The Bible goes on to tell us that, "Knowing this first, that no prophecy of the scripture is of any private interpretation. For the prophecy came not in old time by the will of man: but holy men of God spake as they were moved by the Holy Ghost" (2 Peter 1:20-21).

Genesis 1:1 is the most important verse in the Bible! It is the foundation on which everything else is built. "Even God's great work of salvation is irrelevant and futile without His prior work of creation, for only the Creator of all things could ever become the Savior of all things." Amen! If Genesis is not the foundation, the rest of the Bible ought to be thrown away, too. Two of the most quoted verses in the Bible, "The Lord is my shepherd; I shall not want…" (Psalm 23), and "For God so loved the world that he gave his only begotten Son…" (John 3:16), would be utterly meaningless and become a cliché. It would not matter how many times they are quoted or recited by people in need of comfort.

Even the beloved hymn "Amazing Grace" would also be meaningless. Therefore, the Holy Bible would become an ancient poetry and let all men believe in "Humanist Manifesto II which affirms; No deity will save us; we must save ourselves. Reasonable minds look to other means for survival." Where and how? The Bible warns; "… not to think of yourself more highly than you ought to think…" (Romans 12:3), (Jeremiah 9:23-24). The Bible was not written by unlearned men, as some men have claimed. Listen to how significant the Word of God is, "For thou hath magnified thy word above all thy name" (Psalm 138:2).

Wow! Creationist scientists who believe the Bible have become the object of intense vilification in society, especially in institutions of higher learning. The God of the Bible is the Self-Existent One, the I AM THAT I AM (Exodus 3:14). The Omniscient, the Omnipresent, and the Omnipotent One, who brought everything into existence both animate and inanimate. Is there a book in the libraries of the world that can give such an undisputable and distinctive account of origins? Therefore, the focus of this text will be on the creation of Adam and Eve, our first parents; the myriads of the problems that plague humanity and our civilization today were passed down from them. They are the genesis of man and woman, work, garden, freedom, boundary, sin, doubt, lying and distortion of commandment, disobedience and consequences, dominion mandate, taxonomy, companionship, and marriage, pride, fear, not accepting responsibility, the first gospel, homicide, drunkenness, incest, different tongues and languages (ethnicities), the tower of babel, and the desperate housewife. They are also the Genesis of family feud in Abraham's family (Genesis 21:9-10) and in the house of Jacob (Genesis 37:18-28). The Bible affirms that death is an enemy. "The last enemy that shall be destroyed is death" (1 Corinthians 15:26). There was no death before the fall of Adam. Darwin's philosophy of Survival of the Fittest is a culture of death like the drug culture. Death is not a good thing, but evolutionary humanism is obsessed with death and sees death as a good thing. Listen to Steve Jobs, the founder of Apple Computer in his 2005 commencement address at Sanford University. "Death is very likely the single best invention of Life. It is Life's change agent. It clears out the old to make way for the new."

Is there anyone who would not stop to help someone in an accident, in distress, and fell on a sidewalk? Why not let the person die because he or she is not fit for the society and might not be a contributing member of the society. This would help "clear out the old." Has Steve Jobs ever helped someone? What would cause Steve Jobs or anybody else to think that death is good? "First of all, death came into the world only when sin came into the world. Suffering and death of conscious life whether animal or human, were not a part of God's 'finished' and 'very good' creation (Genesis 1:31). This is an evolutionary philosophy that permeates the educational systems of the world. The God of the Bible is not considered in their thoughts, and they have concluded that He is impersonal and not involved in the affairs of mankind. If He is ever considered, He is considered as "a force or a higher power."

"To effectively tackle a problem, one must know what caused it. A doctor must correctly diagnose a disease to help the sick person get better. If a building collapses, engineers will use root cause analysis to probe with ever-deepening questions of what triggered the accident. Unless the true cause is identified, a professional problem solver is left either treating symptoms or wasting valuable time. A similar approach could be taken with societal ills. What is the root cause of so many of the problems that plague us"? The Bible calls the root cause sin which resulted from Adam's disobedience to clear commands given by God. How, then, can mankind approach societal ills that are ever present with us? Have psychologists and counsellors been treating symptoms and wasting valuable time in trying to solve societal ills without root cause analysis? A few of the societal ills are clearly stated in 2 Timothy 3:2-4. Why do we have the MeToo Movement, why do we have Cheaters Spy Shop, why do we have Partnership for Drug Free America, why do we have Domestic Violence Program, why do we have Mothers Against Drunk Driving, why do we have Betty Ford Clinic, why do we have prisons, and why do we have Alcoholic Anonymous? These are all the legacies of sin.

I thank God for these wonderful organizations trying to solve some of the vexing societal ills. But are they treating symptoms or wasting valuable time? If the root cause is not sin, what then is the root cause? "No gifts or genius or position can keep us safe or from sin." Sin does not respect persons, heritages, zip codes, and nationalities, and it knows no boundaries. It is a pandemic! How many public figures' lives and families did the MeToo Movement and the Illegal Drug Delusion destroy? Is human wisdom alone without wisdom from above sufficient to solve humanities problems?

CHAPTER ONE

Genesis of Man (Male), Woman (Female), and Work

Evolutionary biochemists and other evolutionary scientists have tried for centuries, and they are still trying to resolve how life evolved from non-life or from primitive single cell organisms or from cosmic dust or from primordial soup. Where did they get such an intellect and knowledge to investigate this? Reason without revelation is rubbish. BBC presented "Nature Prehistoric Life, History of Life on Earth." According to this nature program, "The history of life on Earth began about 3.8 billion years ago, initially with single-celled prokaryotic cells, such as bacteria." Who was there to record this? Evolutionary biologists and scientists hold varied views with no definitive resolution as to the origin of man and life. However, if we only have these views without divine revelation, this conundrum can never be resolved. But Glory to God alone (Soli Deo Gloria), He has given us His written Word, the Holy Bible, which clearly testifies that He is the Creator of all things. But the creation record is now the never-ending intellectual debate, but the Bible says, "For this they willingly are ignorant of…" (2 Peter3:5). The Creation account in Genesis to many, learned and unlearned, is a myth, a fairy tale, or a fable.

Now, let us look at who created man and woman. Here God is telling us that He is the Creator and giver of life. "And God said, Let us make man in our own image after our likeness…(God the Father, God the Son, and God the Holy Spirit). So God created man in his own image, in the image of God created he him; male and female created he them" (Genesis 1:26-27). "And the LORD God formed man of the dust of the ground and breathed into his nostrils the breath of life; and man became a living soul"

(Genesis 2:7). God never created man to be idle. Therefore, the genesis of work was introduced. "And the LORD God planted a garden eastward in Eden: and there he put the man whom he had formed" "And the LORD God took the man and put him into the Garden of Eden to dress it and keep it" (Genesis 2:8,15). Adam was given responsibility to take care of the garden and maintain it.

Genesis of the Garden

"And the Lord God planted a garden eastward in Eden; and there he put the man whom he had formed." This references the first garden ever known to mankind. Ever since, there have been myriads of botanical gardens and mansions with elaborate gardens throughout the world. But this garden in Eden has no equal in size and in beauty because the Master Architect designed it and planted it Himself. Listen to this, "And out of the ground made the Lord God to grow every tree that is pleasant to the sight, and good for food; the tree of life also in the midst of the garden, and the tree of knowledge of good and evil" (Genesis 2:8-9). "There was a lovely river to water the garden." This was a perfect garden and a perfect environment without sin where God talked, walked, and communed with Adam and Eve. And it is in this garden that sin came into the world and things fell apart because they could no longer commune with God. Since then, there has been conflict between the flesh and the spirit because the natural man is spiritually "dead in trespasses and sins" (Ephesians 2:1). They are now separated from God, the source of their being. Just unplug your refrigerator from the outlet and see what happens!

"The "flesh," of course, refers to the physical body with all its feelings and appetites, while man's "spirit" refers especially to his spiritual nature with its ability to understand and communicate in terms of spiritual and moral values, along with the potential ability to have a fellowship with God." Then comes the bad news, "For all have sinned and come short of the glory of God (Romans 3:23). Then comes the good news, "Being justified freely by his grace through the redemption that is in Christ" (v. 24). "For as in Adam all die, even so in Christ shall all be made alive" (I Corinthians 15:22). Remember, "they that are in the flesh cannot please God" (Romans 8:8).

Genesis of Freedom, Boundary, and Sin

Freedom is a precious word. It gives people the ability to use their imaginations, to discover and pursue their God-given talents, and to make their visions and dreams come true with little or no restraints. The people of the United States cherish their political, religious, and economic freedoms. There are many countries in the world that deprive its citizens of these freedoms. In any case, the concept of freedom did not originate in ancient Greece, ancient Egypt, ancient Rome, or even in the United States. The word freedom has its origin in the book of Genesis. Adam was not created to be a robot or a puppet; he had a will, lived in a perfect environment, and was free to exercise his will for better or for worse, with obedience or disobedience. God knew that Adam would fall, but He still gave him free will. As human beings, we exercise our will in accordance with or contrary to God's word as Adam did. Adam was the head of mankind, and he freely exercised his will, which was contrary to God's commandment. Therefore, his disobedience plunged the whole human race and the whole earth into all kinds of problems known to mankind.

"A little leaven leaveneth the whole lump" (Galatians 5:9). This is an absolute statement that cannot be denied. In any group there might be one or two people that would do the right thing, but because of peer pressure, they keep silent about the wrong things they see around them. Listen to this; "Be not deceived: evil communications corrupt good manners" (I Corinthians 15:33). Another absolute statement is "Be sure your sin will find you out" (Numbers 32:23). This means that sin, evil behavior, misconduct, and immorality that are tolerated anywhere will eventually become a pandemic. God has these statements as safeguards or checks and balances to prevent these evil deeds. We cannot be wiser than God, who knows the thoughts of all men. Police blue wall of silence was a time-bomb waiting to explode and indeed it exploded.

The MeToo Movement and all of the sex scandals in the Roman Catholic Church, Boys Scouts of America, U.S. Military, U.S.A. Gymnastics, U.S. Olympic Committee, Ivy League Schools, among politicians and lawmakers all ought to cause mankind to cry out to God (and say woe is us) for redemption and salvation! What will make America great again? If America turns back to God and seek first His kingdom and His righteousness (Matthew 6:33).

Listen to this: "This is a faithful saying and worthy of all acceptation, that Christ Jesus came into the world to save sinners" (I Timothy 1:15). Wow! The above listed scandals started out one at a time, and they kept growing and growing, but those in authority were complacent and allowed perpetrators or abusers to continue their criminal behaviors without holding anyone accountable or punishing them. In our wisdom, we think we can handle or control anything without regard to warnings, which then leads to our own shameful and deadly realities as we see them today. It is a fallacy to think that those in uniforms and those who wear academic gowns are beyond reproach. Is man's wisdom alone sufficient to know what is in the heart of man without divine revelation? "Sin and death are grim realities in the world."

"And the Lord God commanded the man, saying, 'of every tree of the garden thou mayest freely eat: But of the tree of the knowledge of good and evil, thou shalt not eat of it: for in the day that thou eatest thereof thou shalt surely die" (Genesis 2:16-17). Human beings are the crown jewels of God's creations because only human beings bear His image. God gave detailed and clear commandments to Adam. Even though we live in an enlightened and technologically advanced society, we are being deceived as Eve was deceived. Therefore, mankind cannot solve societal ills with man's wisdom alone.

There must be wisdom from above and divine revelation! "Now the serpent was more subtle than any beast of the field which the LORD God had made. And he said unto the woman, 'Yea, hath God said, ye shall not eat of every tree of the garden.' And the woman said unto the serpent, 'We may eat of the fruit of the trees of the garden. But of the fruit of the tree which is in the midst of the garden, God hath said, Ye shall not eat of it, neither shall ye touch it, lest ye die.' And the serpent our ancient foe, said unto the woman, Ye shall not surely die,'" (Genesis 3:1-4). Wow! God's commandment was given in a clear language without ambiguity and ought to have been taken literary, but Adam and Eve chose not to take it literary. They accepted Satan's non-literal interpretation.

The debate today, even in some Christian schools and congregations, is whether or not the creation account in Genesis and the Genesis flood record should be taken literary? The other debate whether or not the Lord Jesus Christ is the only way to God (John 14:6). Is this to be taken literary or not? It is very deadly and dangerous to interpret Scriptures to fit one's own preferences. Please remember Galatians 5:9: "And when the woman saw that the tree was good for food, and that it was pleasant to the eyes (the lust of the eyes), and a tree desired to make one wise (pride of life). She took of the fruit and did eat, (the lust of the flesh) and gave also unto her husband with her and he did eat. And the eyes of both were opened, and they knew that they were naked; and they sewed fig leaves together and made themselves aprons" (Genesis 3:6-7). They were now conscious of sin and moral guilt.

Do you see the effects of sin? The fig leaves they used to cover themselves is the genesis of human efforts to cover for their sins. Today, we reject the covering of God in the Lord Jesus Christ and go about covering ourselves in the form of good deeds! I am in favor of doing good, but let us not boast of our good works and only boast of His finished work on the Cross! Please remember, the arm of the flesh will always fail us! Human wisdom, philosophy, capitalism, democratic ideals, or any system of government cannot save any nation! Did the Enlightenment Era of the late 1700s draw the U.S. or any other nation closer to the God of the Bible, or did it push us further away?

The Man Born Blind, Sovereignty of God
"And his disciples asked him, saying, 'Master who did sin, this man, or

his parents, that he was born blind?' Jesus answered, 'Neither hath this man sinned, nor his parents: but that the works of God should be made manifest in him" (John 9:2-3). Pay attention to this part of the Scripture: "Nay but, O man, who art thou that repliest against God? Shall the thing formed say to him that formed it, why hast thou made me thus? Hath not the potter power over the clay, of the same lump to make one vessel unto honour, and another unto dishonour?" (Romans 9:20-21)

"Mankind has always found it easy to fall into the trap of thinking that suffering of any sort is due to sin. To be sure, much suffering is due to sin, and even after repentance and forgiveness, scars may remain. If there had been no sin, there would have been no suffering." "But now, O LORD, thou art our father; we are the clay, and thou our potter; and we all are the work of thy hand" (Isaiah 64:8). I don't know how God gets glory in this story, or in any other situation, but He does!

Genesis of Doubt, Lying and Distortion of Commandment
Eve knows the commandment God gave to Adam. Perhaps the serpent knows that Adam would not be easily persuaded, so he first went to Eve. "Now the serpent was more subtle than any beast of the field which the LORD God had made. And he said unto the woman, 'Yea, hath God said, ye shall not eat of every tree of the garden?' And the woman said unto the serpent, 'We may eat of the fruit of the trees of the garden. But of the fruit of the tree which is in the midst of the garden, God hath said, Ye shall not eat of it, neither shall ye touch it, lest ye die.' And the serpent said unto the woman, 'Ye shall not surely die'" (Genesis 3:1-4).

"Our ancient foe, doth seek to work us woe, his craft and power are great, and armed with cruel hate, on earth is not his equal." "For God doth know that in the day ye eat thereof, then your eyes shall be opened, and ye shall be as gods, knowing good and evil. Yea, hath God said?" In order words, does God always means exactly what he says in His word? Or is there a grey area? "The Devil's tactics change with time and culture, but the strategy remains the same. First, Satan always attempts to make us doubt the Word of God" (v.1). The devil's tactics can be called the three Ds strategy: Doubt, Denial, and Denigration."

The fact is that when you begin to doubt what follows next, you are questioning the infallibility and sufficiency of all scriptures (2 Timothy 3:16). "Second, Satan always confronts the doubter with a denial of the Word of God (v.4). Third, Satan ultimately heaps denigration on the Person of God Himself (v.5). That the Word of God is not trustworthy, and that God either will not or cannot do what He says." Therefore, you are calling God a liar. This then leads to doubt, which then leads to denial and then lying, and then the distortion of clear commandments without ambiguity.

The commandments never said anything about touch. "Neither shall ye touch it" (v.4). Abraham lied about his wife Sarah (Genesis 20:2). Isaac also lied about his wife Rebekah (Genesis 26:7). After the death of Joseph's father, his brother's conscience pricked them, and they felt guilty of the evil they did unto him. Therefore, they concocted a lie to save themselves. "And they sent a messenger unto Joseph, saying, Thy father did command before he died, saying, So shall ye say unto Joseph, Forgive, I pray thee now, the trespass of thy brethren, and their sin; for they did unto thee evil: the trespass of the servants of the God of thy father" (Genesis 50:16-17). "…And be sure your sin will find you out" (Numbers 32:23). No gift or genius or position can keep us safe from sin.

CHAPTER TWO

Genesis Flood and Grace

The deluge of Noah's day is as controversial as Genesis 1:1 and the creation account. God used this deluge to judge the world then, and everything that had breath perished. Skeptics call it a local flood. Is it possible for a local flood to alter the landscapes of the world? In order to understand the deluge of Noah's day, root cause analysis is necessary to identify the true cause. "And the LORD said, My spirit shall not always strive with man." (Genesis 6:3) God's assessment of the human heart was very bad. (Proverbs 4:23 warning, Jeremiah 17:9 wicked, and Matthew15:18-19). Listen to this; "And God saw that the wickedness of man was great in the earth, and that every imagination of the thoughts of his heart was only evil continually" (Genesis 6:5). Wow!

"And the LORD said, I will destroy man whom I have created from the face of the earth; both man, and beast, and the creeping things, and fowls of the air; for it repented me that I have made man. But Noah found grace in the eyes of the LORD. And God looked down upon the earth, and, behold, it was corrupt, for all flesh had corrupted his way upon the earth. Earth is center of God's interest in the universe. And God said unto Noah, 'The end of all flesh is come before me; for the earth is filled with violence through them; and, behold, I will destroy them with the earth'" (vv. 7, 8, 12-13). God commanded Noah to build an ark, and he obeyed the Lord and did as he was commanded. When the fullness of time came, "And Noah went in, and his sons, and his wife, and his sons' wives with him into the ark" (Genesis 7:8-9). And two of every creature, both clean and unclean, went in also.

9

"The same day were all the fountains of the great deep broken up, and the windows of heaven were opened" (v. 11). "And the waters prevailed exceedingly upon the earth; and all the hills, that were under the whole heaven were covered." Fifteen cubits, about twenty-two feet upward, did the waters prevail; and the mountains were covered. And all flesh died that moved upon the earth, both of fowl, and of cattle, and of beast, and of every creeping thing that creepeth upon the earth and every man. All in whose nostrils was the breath of life, of all that was in the dry land died… Noah only remained alive, and they that were with him in the ark" (vv.19-23). Listen to Apostle Peter under the inspiration of the Holy Spirit, "For this they willingly are ignorant of, that by the word of God the heavens were of old, and the earth standing out of the water and in the water: Whereby the world that then was being overflowed with water perished" (2 Peter 3:5-6). They were willingly ignorant back then, and today majority of people are also willingly ignorant!

Genesis of Disobedience and Consequences

Adam completely disobeyed God and allowed Satan to deceive him. "So he drove out the man; and he placed at the east of the garden of Eden Cherubims, and a flaming sword which turned every way, to keep the way of the tree of life" (Genesis 3:24)." Ever since Adam and Eve brought sin into the world, everybody born has an innate rebellion against God." Listen to this: "The wicked are estranged from the womb: they go astray as soon as they be born, speaking lies" (Psalm 58:3). "The image of God in man has been grievously marred. Hence, we are dead in trespasses and sins" (Ephesians 2:1). Sin is the deadliest pandemic in the world because it knows no boundaries! This is the genesis of intellectual battle between Adam's children and Satan.

This ancient deception is now a modern intellectual battle that has been going on for centuries, and it is yet to be abated. Deists believe in the existence of a Supreme being, such as a Creator, but they don't believe that the Creator intervenes in the universe. Theists believe that there is God who made and governs all creations, but they don't believe in the doctrine of the Trinity nor in divine revelation. According to the Bible, both Deists and Theists are wrong! The deluge of Noah's day is God's intervention in the universe because of sin. The word trinity is not found in the bible, but it is implied. "…these three are one" (I John 5:7).

"In the beginning God created the heaven and the earth" (Genesis 1:1). God revealed to Noah that He was going to destroy man and all his creations on the earth with flood. Therefore, he was instructed to build an Ark! (Genesis 6:13). "The spirit of the LORD spake by me, and his word was in my tongue" (II Samuel 23:2). According to the Scriptures, Deists and Theists "are without excuse" (Romans 1:20). "They willingly are ignorant" (II Peter3:5). As a matter of fact, *The King James Authorized Bible* has 783,137 words. These words are Divine Revelations."

If there is no divine revelation, let us then look to the heavenly bodies of the stars, the moon, and the sun in order to solve problems of mankind. There are no two ways about this; either you are in Adam or in Christ; either you believe and trust God's account of creation or you believe and trust evolutionary philosophers and scientists. It is all or nothing! This is God's absolute standard! "For as by one man's disobedience many were made sinners, so by the obedience of one shall many be made righteous" (Romans 5:19). "As the elders said, if one finger brought oil it soiled the others." "For as in Adam all die, [Bad News] even so in Christ shall all be made alive [Good News]" (1 Corinthians 15:22).

In Genesis (2:16-17), the Lord God gave precise and clear commandment to Adam and the consequences that would follow suit if he did not obey. Adam was tested to obey or not to obey. Adam and Eve were given freedom to eat any fruit they want except one. There is a consequence in either belief. "There is a way which seemeth right unto a man, but the end thereof are the ways of death" (Proverbs 14:12). This way of man has no wisdom, no safety, no hope, no assurance of salvation, and does not show the right way to go. According to Psalm 119, the word of God gives wisdom and understanding (vv.98-100, 130, hope (v.166), and it shows a pathway with light (v.105). It is God and God alone who spoke, and things came into existence. Listen to this; "And God said, 'Let there be light and there was light'" (Genesis 1:3). "All things were made by him; and without him was not anything made that was made" (John 1:3).

Genesis of Curse Imposed by God

Are the people of the twenty-first century more obedient than Adam and Eve or any other generation? Adam ought to have kept and guarded the commandment he received from God, but when he was confronted, he blamed Eve and, ultimately, blamed God. Listen to what he said, "And the man said, 'The woman whom thou gavest to be with me, she gave me of the tree and I did eat.' And the LORD God said unto the woman, 'What is this that thou hast done?' And the woman said, 'The serpent beguiled me and I did eat'. And the Lord God said unto the serpent 'Because thou hast done this, thou art cursed…I will put enmity between thee and the woman, and between they seed and her seed; it shall bruise thy head, and thou shalt bruise his heel.' Unto the woman He said, 'I will greatly multiply thy sorrow and thy conception.' And unto Adam He said, 'Because thou hast hearkened unto the voice of thy wife, and hath eaten of the tree of which I commanded thee…cursed is the ground for thy sake...Thorns also and thistles shall it bring forth to thee. In the sweat of thy face shalt thou eat bread, till thou return unto the ground'" (Genesis 3:12-19).

Unfortunately, the serpent had no one to blame. We live in an era where we can always find someone or something to blame, such as TV ads, video games, peer pressure, dysfunctional families, and so on. I know how powerful temptations are, and I am not trying to make light of them. We can no longer master temptations or trials in our own strength and power, because we are no longer in our rightful minds due to the fall of man. God cursed His very good creations, "All of creations were placed under the curse of death, the animals (v.14), the ground (v.17), and mankind (v.19)." Then, work becomes difficult, and thorns and thistles begin to grow, and then pestilences, famine, and diseases come. They go from epidemic to pandemic! The curse is echoed in the New Testament. "For the creation was made subject to vanity, not willingly, but reason of him who hath subjected the same in hope, Because the creature itself also shall be delivered from the bondage of corruption into the glorious liberty of the children of God. For we know that the whole creation groaneth and travaileth in pain together until now" (Romans 8:20-22).

CHAPTER THREE

Genesis of Dominion Mandate

Dominion has to do with control, taking charge, or ruling. The control man has over creatures in a circus is amazing. Even the most dangerous beast in the wild has been under man's control. This was a mandate given to man by God. This is shown in Genesis, "And God said, let us make man in our image, after our likeness: and let them have dominion over the fish of the sea, and over the fowl of the air, and over the cattle, and over all the earth, and over every creeping thing that creepeth upon the earth" (Genesis 1:26). Because of this dominion mandate, man has been able to do things such as deep-sea mining and outer-space explorations. I have never tamed any creature, but it must have taken hours to tame wild and dangerous creatures. Even though man has tamed every known creature, there is one thing that man cannot tame, according to the word of God. Listen to this, "For every kind of beast, and of birds, and of serpents, and of things in the sea, is tamed, and hath been tamed of mankind. But the tongue can no man tame; it is an unruly evil, full of deadly poison" (James 3:7-8). This was written centuries before modern psychology.

No man could have known this except, God. Many people have regretted what they have said, and this is a common occurrence. The usual response whenever it happens is, "I do not mean to say it that way. My statement was taken out of context, and I do not mean to offend anyone. I am not that kind of a person." Really? Whatever you said came out of your heart. The Scripture tells us, "Keep thy heart with all diligence; for out of it are the issues of life" (Proverbs 4:23). "Not that

15

which goeth into the mouth defileth a man; but that which cometh out of the mouth that defileth a man" (Matthew 15 :11). "The thoughts of our hearts will inevitably control the words on our lips and the works of our hands." How is it that the fiercest creatures known to mankind has been tamed, but the tongue cannot be tamed? It is because God had declared it be so, and, thus, no drug or counseling can tame the tongue. The absolute truth is that our mouths are connected to our hearts. This is an undisputable statement.

Genesis of Taxonomy, Companionship, and Institution of Marriage
"Taxonomy is the process of naming and classifying things such as animals and plants." Ernst Mayr, a 20th century evolutionary biologist, was not the first taxonomist: Adam was the first. "And out of the ground the LORD God formed every beast of the field, and every fowl of the air; and brought them unto Adam to see what he would call them: and whatsoever Adam called every living creation, that was the name thereof. And Adam gave names to all cattle, and to the fowl of the air, and to every beast of the field; but for Adam there was not found an help meet for him" (Genesis 2:19-20). God knows that Adam needed a companion because in all the beasts of the field, there was none like Adam. Adam did not say to the chimpanzee, "this is bone of my bones and flesh of my flesh," because he knows that he is not a close relative of a chimpanzee or ape.

Listen to this; "And the LORD God said, it is not good that the man should be alone; I will make him an help meet for him" (v.18). This was the genesis of the first surgery and the institution of marriage. "And the LORD God caused a deep sleep to fall upon Adam, and he slept: and he took one of his ribs… And the rib, which the LORD God had taken from man, made he a woman, and brought her unto the man." What an excitement! "And Adam said, 'This is now bone of my bones, and flesh of my flesh: she shall be called Woman, because she was taken out of Man.' Therefore, shall a man leave his father and his mother, and shall cleave unto his wife: and they shall be one flesh" (vv. 21-24).

Genesis of Pride

Webster's Dictionary defines Pride as; "A sense of one's own proper value or dignity; self-respect." I don't think there is anything wrong in being proud of one's accomplishments. However, pride that is contemptible of others is contrary to the Bible. Pride in one's heart that has no regard for God or fear of God is always dangerous! Listen to what the Bible says about pride, "Everyone that is proud in heart is an abomination to the LORD" (Proverbs 16:5). "Pride goeth before destruction, and an haughty spirit before a fall" (v.18). Martin Luther called Satan "our ancient foe." God created Lucifer, the highest ranking of the angelic hosts. In a modern language, he was the Chief of Staff. Angels are created beings to serve the Lord God and worship him. Satan is the same as the Devil. He is not omnipotent, omnipresent, and omniscient. However, he is the angel of darkness and a master deceiver. He and his cohorts have diabolic plans to destroy mankind. Satan was not content with his status in heaven, and he rebelled against His Creator. He had a free will to serve and worship God, his Creator, but he chose to rebel instead.

The same was true for our first parents, Adam and Eve. The free will God gave them has potential for sin, but God is sovereign over Satan. The sin in the Garden of Eden was not a surprise to God. It was God's pleasure for Christ to pay the penalty for the sins of us all. "Declaring the end from the beginning, and from ancient times the things that are not yet done, saying, My counsel shall stand, and I will do all my pleasure" (Isaiah 46:10). "But he was wounded for our transgressions, he was bruised for our iniquities: the chastisement of our peace was upon him, and with his strips we are healed. …the LORD hath laid on him the iniquity of us all" (Isaiah 53:5-6).

God created Adam and Eve as perfect beings. However, Satan knows that one day, God is going to cast him and his angels into a lake of fire. Therefore, he is relentlessly in pursuit of turning many people away from God. Heed this warning, "Be sober, be vigilant; because your adversary the devil, as a lion walketh about seeking whom he may devour" (1 Peter 5:8). Listen again, "And no marvel; for Satan himself is transformed into an angel of light" (II Corinthians 11:14). Satan started this with our first parents, Adam and Eve. The perpetual questions today are about the genesis of sin in the world, the evil in the world, and the works of Satan in the world.

However, the real question is, are these things real and true? Is there any man or institution out there that can resolve these vexing issues? Do we take God at His word, or do we follow our own devices or interpret the Scriptures to fit our own preferences? However, Lucifer was not content to serve and worship God as he was created to do. Therefore, he became prideful and rebelled against his Creator. A third of the angelic beings followed him. Pride always glorifies self and not God! Our ancient foe's favorite tool is pride. Pride is self-oriented, ego-driven, and has desire for dominance, contempt for others, and supremacy. This was the reason Satan lost his exalted position.

Listen to what God said, "How art thou fallen from heaven, O Lucifer, son of the morning! *How* art thou cut down to the ground, which didst weaken the nations! For thou hast said in thine heart, I will ascend into heaven, I will exalt my throne above the stars of God: I will sit upon the mount of the congregation in the sides of the north: I will ascend above the heights of the cloud; I will be like the most High. Yet thou shalt be brought down to hell, to the sides of the pit" (Isaiah 14:12-15). "The thoughts of our hearts will inevitably control the words on our lips and the works of our hands." Is there a human being that is without pride?

The reason why the human race was plunged into sin was the pride of Eve. Satan appealed to her in the garden, and she fell. (Genesis 3:6). He also tempted Christ in the wilderness (Luke 4:6). What about today? Our ancient foe has not changed his modus operandi. There is no human being that is his equal. Therefore, the Bible warned; "God resisteth the proud, but giveth grace unto the humble" (James 4:6). If you try to lift yourself up like Satan, God will certainly bring you down! Therefore, "Humble yourself in the sight of the Lord, and he shall lift you up" (v.10). This is a promise!

Remember Nebuchadnezzar? Listen to what he said; "The King spake, and said, 'Is not this great Babylon, that I have built for the house of the kingdom by the might of my power, and for the honour of my majesty?' While the word was in the king's mouth, there fell a voice from heaven, saying, 'O king Nebuchadnezzar to thee it is spoken; The kingdom is departed from thee'" (Daniel 4:30-31). He did not give God glory, but himself, "…For without me ye can do nothing" (John 15:5). However, God did not let him get away and he was driven out into the field and ate grass like the beast of the fields (vv.32-33). Wow! There are a lot of Nebuchadnezzars in the world today, but because of God's longsuffering, they continue to live and see themselves as immortal deities, intoxicated with power, and have no fear of God before their eyes. "When I thought to know this, it was too painful for me; Until I went into the sanctuary of God; then understood I their end" (Psalms 73:16-17).

CHAPTER FOUR

Genesis of Fear

Prior to the fall in the garden, there was no fear or shame, even though Adam and Eve were both naked. "There was no need for shame at their lack of clothing for neither had any consciousness of sin or moral guilt." They gave into Satan's greatest lie, "Ye shall not surely die." Then they ate the fruit, and their eyes were opened "and they knew that they were naked; and they sewed fig leaves together and made themselves aprons" (Genesis 3:7). "And the LORD God called unto Adam, and said unto him, 'Where art thou?'" (v.9). They have heard the voice of the LORD God before and never hid themselves from His presence. When He called on Adam, his reply was "I heard thy voice in the garden, and I was afraid, because I was naked; and I hid myself" (v.10). They are now conscious of sin and moral guilt, and they immediately sewed fig leaves to cover themselves. Thus, they can no longer present themselves faultless before God. This is also true today that nobody can stand before God on his or her own merits or good deeds.

Genesis of Not Accepting Responsibility (Passing the Buck)

Adam and Eve disobeyed God in the Garden of Eden! God gave them commandment that was clear, precise, and without ambiguity. Listen to the command: "And the LORD God commanded the man, saying 'Of every tree of the garden thou mayest freely eat: But of the tree of the knowledge of good and evil, thou shall not eat of it: for in the day that thou eatest thereof thou shall surely die'" (Genesis 2:16-17). Listen to this contradiction, "Now the serpent was more subtle than any beast of the field which the LORD God had made. And he said unto the woman, Yea, hath had God said, 'Ye shall not eat of every tree of the garden?'" (Genesis 3:1) "And the woman said unto the serpent, 'We may eat of the fruit of the trees of the garden: But of the fruit of the tree which is in the midst of the garden, God hath said, Ye shall not eat of it, neither shall ye touch it, lest ye die.' And the serpent said unto the woman, 'Ye shall not surely die'" (vv3-4) Ever since the fall of Adam, mankind has determined not to accept full responsibility of guilt. Eve was deceived by Satan, and she ate the fruit and gave it to Adam. When the Lord God later came, he called unto Adam "and said unto him, 'Where art thou'"? (v 9).

Adam was held responsible, not Eve, because he was the head of family and the head of humanity. God asked him, "Hast thou eaten of the tree, whereof I commanded thee that thou shouldest not eat?" "And the man said, 'The woman whom thou gavest to be with me, she gave me of the tree, and I did eat.' And the LORD God said unto the woman, 'What is this that thou hath done?' And the woman said, 'The serpent beguiled me, and I did eat.'" This is known as the domino effect in modern language. "And the LORD God said unto the serpent, 'Because thou hath done this, thou art cursed above all cattle, and above every beast of the field: upon thy belly shalt thou eat all the days of thy life'" (Genesis 3:11-14). The disobedience of Adam marred the relationship between man and God! It also caused spiritual separation between them, and man can no longer commune with God.

Companies pay huge fines without accepting responsibility of any wrongdoing. The people of the 21st Century are more sophisticated and pride themselves in wisdom, knowledge, and in advanced technologies. But are we different from Adam and Eve? No! We have not renounced the hidden things of dishonesty, we have not renounced walking in craftiness, we have not renounced walking with pride, and we have not renounced handling the word of God deceitfully!

Genesis of the First Gospel (Protoevangelium)
Protoevangelium is a compound of two Greek words, pronto meaning "first" and evangelion meaning "good news" or "gospel." Therefore, the good news

or the gospel had its origin in the Book of Genesis. In a nutshell, this good news starts from the Book of Genesis to the Book of Revelation and how God's plan of redemption will be fulfilled in the Lord Jesus Christ in the New Testament. However, it is the genesis of spiritual warfare between the seed of the woman and the seed of the serpent. Listen to this: "And the LORD God said unto the serpent, because thou hath done this, thou art cursed above all cattle, and above every beast of the field; upon thy belly shalt thou go, and dust shalt thou eat all the days of thy life. And I will put enmity between thee and the woman, and between thy seed and her seed; it shall bruise thy head, and thou shall bruise his heel" (Genesis 3:14-15). This battle will go on until the second coming of the Lord Jesus Christ.

Satan "our ancient foe" will continue to oppose the Gospel because he is the father of lies and will do anything to keep many people from taking heed to this wonderful message. "This is a faithful saying, and worthy of all acceptation, that Christ Jesus came into the world to save sinners" (1 Timothy 1:15). This message was not worthy of complete acceptance to many ancient evolutionary intellectuals and philosophers. It is also true today of many modern evolutionary intellectuals and philosophers in all disciplines. Adam and Eve covered themselves with fig leaves. Today, many people are covering themselves with their good works.

It is God who has placed any good deed in the heart of humanity. But can anybody stand before the God of all creations on his or her own merits without the Cross? The seed of the woman is none other the Lord Jesus Christ, the Chief Shepherd. The prophecy of Prophet Isaiah 53 was all about Jesus Christ. "All we like sheep have gone astray; we have turned everyone to his own way; and the LORD hath laid on him the iniquity of us all" (Isaiah 53:6)."Who verily was foreordained before the foundation of the world, but was manifest in these last times for you" (I Peter 1:20). "…The Lamb slain from the foundation of the world" (Revelation 13:8). When sin entered into the world, humanity fell into bondage at the hands of Satan. "Wherefore, as by one man, sin entered into the world, and death by sin, and so death passed upon all men, for that all have sinned" (Romans 5:12).

Sin has separated us from God as it separated Adam and Eve from God. Listen to this wonderful statement: "But God commendeth his love toward us, in that, while we were yet sinners, Christ died for us" (v. 8). "For as in Adam all die, [the bad news] even so in Christ shall all be made alive" [the good news] (I Corinthians 15:22).

Genesis of God's Intervention in Human Lives
In Genesis chapter four, we have the story of Adam and Eve having children, who we know as Cain and Abel. Cain was a farmer, a tiller of the ground, and Abel was a keeper of sheep. They both knew about making a sacrifice unto the Lord. But when the time came to make sacrifice, "Cain brought of the fruit of the ground an offering unto the LORD. And Abel he also brought of the firstlings of his flock and of the fat thereof. And the LORD had respect unto Abel and to his offering" (Genesis 4:3-4). Adam and Eve knew of the commandment of the Lord God, and they willingly disobeyed. Cain and Abel knew what type of offering was acceptable unto the Lord. Cain decided to do it his way by offering fruits of the ground instead of an animal sacrifice.

It is true that he gave the Lord what he had. However, it was not the required offering. Did he forget that the sacrifice had to be an animal? He tried to do it his way. Doing it your way has deadly consequences. The Scripture tells us that, "But unto Cain and to his offering he had not respect. And Cain was very wroth, and his countenance fell. Anger that is not controlled will inevitably lead to a tragedy! And the LORD said unto Cain, 'Why art thou wroth? And why is thy countenance fallen? If thou doest well, shalt thou not be accepted? And if thou doest not well, sin lieth at the door. And unto thee shall be his desire, and thou shalt rule over him'" (vv.5-7). Almighty God himself pleaded with Cain to do the right thing. If he forgot, he now knew what to do. He could have gone to his brother and asked him to give him a flock to make his offering. But he was very wroth with the Lord and it spilled over to his brother. We do not set the standard or tell God what is acceptable. He and He alone sets the standard and tells us what is acceptable. Perhaps, he was too proud to go to his brother and ask for help. Today, too many people do it their way and say something like, "All religions lead to God," or "You cannot put God in a box."

Is there anyone who works for a company that does not follow company rules, policies, and regulations? Or is there anyone who does not follow manufacturer's manual to assemble or operate a machine? Please listen to this, "Enter ye in the strait gate: for wide is the gate, and broad is the way, that leadeth to destruction, and many there be which go in thereat: Because strait is the gate, and narrow is the way, which leadeth unto life, and few there be that find it" (Matthew 7:13-14). The narrow way is the Lord Jesus Christ! "There is a way that seemeth right unto a man, but the end thereof are the ways of death" (Proverbs 14:12). Take heed (I Timothy 4:16). Beware (Matthew 7:15). Absolute truth does not depend on majority opinions and cannot be debated. Please remember Adam and Eve, and do not try to do it your way!

CHAPTER FIVE

*Genesis of Homicide (Cain slew his brother Abel and
murder plot by Joseph's brothers)*

"And Cain talked with Abel his brother: and it came to pass, when they
were in the field, that Cain rose up against Abel his brother and slew him.
"And the LORD said unto Cain, 'Where is Abel thy brother?' And he said,
'I know not: Am I my brother's keeper?' And he said, 'What hast thou
done? the voice of thy brother's blood crieth unto me from the ground"
(Genesis 4:8-10). There is nothing that is hidden from the face of the Lord.
"The eyes of the LORD are in every place, beholding the evil and the good"
(Proverbs 15:3). "For his eyes are upon the ways of man, and he seeth all
his goings. There is no darkness, nor shadow of death where the workers
of iniquity may hide themselves" (Job 34:21-22).

How could this homicide happen in an environment with only four
people? Was this a case of racism? Was this a case of poverty, lack of
education, lack of employment, an absentee father, proliferation of guns, or
drugs? This is part of the spiritual warfare and the plot of Satan, our ancient
foe, is to steal, kill, and destroy life. Since the fall of Adam, the heart of man
has become deceitful and desperately wicked. Politicians, lawmakers, and
citizens are looking for answers to bring about a change for people to live
together without hatred and violence! Thank God; only He can show the
human race how wicked our hearts are. The thoughts of our hearts will
inevitably control the words on our lips and the works of our hands.

Listen to God's assessment of the human heart! "And God saw that
the wickedness of man was great in the earth, and that every imagination
of the thoughts of his heart was only evil continually" (Genesis 6:5). "Yea

in heart ye work wickedness, ye weigh the violence of your hands in the earth. The wicked are estranges from the womb: they go astray as soon as they be born, speaking lies. Their poison is like the poison of a serpent: they are like the deaf adder that stopped her ear" (Psalm 58:2-4). "Their feet run to evil, and they make haste to shed innocent blood: their thoughts are thoughts of iniquity; wasting and destruction are in their paths" (Isaiah 59:7) "The heart is deceitful above all things, and desperately wicked: who can know it?" (Jeremiah 17:9). With all these uncomfortable assessments of the human heart, why do humans have the capacity to do good deeds? Evolutionary biologists, evolutionary anthropologists, and evolutionary philosophers have been trying to understand what makes a human a human. Humans are created in the image of God (Genesis 1:27).

However, evolutionists tell us that we are here because of Big Bang. Humans are not cousins of chimpanzees! The Bible clearly states in Genesis 1 that God created everything "after his kind." Even though sin has marred the relationship between man and God, man still has some capacity to do good deeds, such as generosity, self-sacrifice, kindness, etc.! Abraham lied to King Abimelech about his wife Sarah being his sister. Sarah also said that Abraham was her brother. Therefore, the king took Sarah. He took her to do what? I believe he took Sarah to go into her "the lust of the eyes" and "the lust of the flesh." "But God came to Abimelech in a dream by night, and said to him, 'Behold, thou art but a dead man, for the woman which thou hath taken; for she is a man's wife'" (Genesis 20:3). The Bible forbids fornication. If men are hearing God's voice like this, there would have been no fornication in the world! He said that he took Sarah in the integrity of his heart, and he was innocent. In this case, he applied situational ethics. But does the Bible allow the application of situational ethics in life?

"And God said unto him in a dream, Yes, I know that thou didst this in the integrity of thy heart; for I also withheld thee from sinning against me: therefore suffered I thee not to touch her" (v.6). "And Judah said unto his brethren, What profit is it if we slay our brother, and conceal his blood?

Come let us sell him to the Ish-mee-lites and let not our hand be upon him; for he is our brother and our flesh. And his brethren were content" (Genesis 37:26-27). How does this diabolic plan to murder their brother take a turn for good? "And Joseph said unto them, 'Fear not: for am I in the place of God? But as for you, ye thought evil against me; but God meant it unto good...to save much people alive'" Genesis 50:19-20). God has been accused of not being all-powerful and unable to intervene to stop all evil deeds in the world.

Here is a question for those contending with God, "Shall he that contendeth with the Almighty instruct him? he that reproveth God, let him answer it" (Job 40:2). This is the world's greatest mystery that theologians and philosophers have yet to answer. But the above examples clearly show the sovereignty of God! He does not answer to any man and does "all things after the counsel of his own will" (Ephesians 1:11). "Nay but, O man, who art thou that repliest against God? Shall the thing formed say to him that formed it, 'Why hast thou made me thus? Hath not the potter power over the clay, of the same lump to make one vessel unto honour, and another unto dishonour?'" (Romans 9:20-21). As a matter of fact, the whole chapter of Romans 9 is about the sovereignty of God. Have we not rejected the foundational teaching of creation and held onto evolution? Unless we know the root cause of our problems, we will continue to go through a revolving door!

Humanity has more than enough knowledge of atrocities in the world, and yet these atrocities continue to go on. How do we then make reconciliation a reality and eliminate disparity? "A more perfect Union" in the constitution cannot happen with just civil conversations! The wisdom of the world and its pragmatic prudence are incapable in themselves to bring about reconciliation! And there is no death of a sinful mortal being that can reconcile humanity, especially in the United States! "I am the vine, and ye are the branches: He that abideth in me, and I in him, the same bringeth forth much fruit: for without me ye can do nothing" (John 15:5). "And all things are of God, who hath reconciled us to himself by Jesus

Christ, and hath given to us the ministry of reconciliation" (II Corinthians 5:18). If God has not revealed Himself in nature's creation and in the Lord Jesus Christ when the Word became flesh, I will say that one day, we will be able to pull ourselves up by our bootstraps!

"For the invisible things of him from creation of the world are clearly seen, being understood by the things that are made, even his eternal power and Godhead; so they are without excuse. Because that, when they knew God, they glorified him not as God, neither were thankful; but became vain in their imaginations, and their foolish heart was darkened. Professing themselves to be wise, they became fools" (Romans1:20-22). We are completely disconnected from our source, the God who created all things. Christ is the giver of life, and Satan is the destroyer of life. Satan is not a figment of man's imagination to scare people. Please do not be deceived, Satan does not have horns and does not wear a red suit with a pitchfork in his hand. He is a created spiritual being, and he is the adversary of mankind. Therefore, the Bible warns; "Be sober, be vigilant; because your adversary the devil, as a roaring lion walketh about, seeking whom he may devour" (I Peter 5:8). Mankind does not have power, wisdom, knowledge, and the intellect to defeat Satan! But to whom shall we go?

Martin Luther tells us:
"For still our ancient foe.
Doth seek to work us woe;
His craft and power are great,
And armed with cruel hate,
On earth is not his equal.
Did we in our own strength confide,
Our striving would be losing;
Were not the right man on our side
Doth ask who that may be?
Christ Jesus it is He!
Amen and Amen!"

Genesis of Drunkenness and Incest

God made a covenant with Noah after the flood. "And God blessed Noah and his sons, and said unto them, 'Be fruitful, and multiply, and replenish the earth'" (Genesis 9:1). "And I will remember my covenant, which is between me and you and every living creature of all flesh: and the waters shall no more become a flood to destroy all flesh" (v.15). "And Noah began to be a husbandman, and he planted a vineyard: And he drank of the wine, was drunken; and he was uncovered within his tent. And Ham, the father of Canaan, saw the nakedness of his father, and told his two brothers without. And Shem and Japhet took a garment, and laid it upon both shoulders, and went backward, and covered the nakedness of their father; and their faces were backward, and they saw not their father's nakedness. And Noah awoke from his wine, and knew what his younger son had done unto him" (vv.20-24).

After the destruction of Sodom and Gomorrah, Lot and his two daughters went with him to dwell in Zoar. "And the first born said unto the younger, 'Our father is old, and there is not a man in the earth to come in unto us after the manner of all the earth: Come, let us make our father drink wine, and we will lie with him, that we may preserve seed of our father.' And they made their father drink wine that night: and the first born went in, and lay with her father; and he perceived not when she lay down, nor when she arose. And it came to pass on the morrow, that the firstborn said unto the younger, Behold, I lay yesternight with my father. Thus were both the daughters of Lot with child by their father" (Genesis 19:31-36).

Genesis of Seduction, Rape, and the Power of Ungodly Friend

Since the entrance of sin into the world, the immorality and moral decadence have been unspeakable! Amnon, the son of King David, raped his sister. "And it came to pass after this, that Absalom the son of David had a fair sister, whose name was Tamar; and Amnon the son of David loved her. And Amnon was so vexed that he fell sick for his sister Tamar; for she was a virgin; and Amnon thought it hard for him to do anything to her. Amnon had a friend whose name was Jonadab…and Jonadab was a very subtle man. And he said unto him, 'Why art thou, being the king's son, lean from day to day? Wilt thou not tell?' And Amnon said unto him, 'I love Tamar, my brother Absalom's sister.' And Jonadab said unto him, 'Lay thee down on thy bed, and make thyself sick: and when thy father cometh to see thee, say unto him, I pray thee, let my sister Tamar come, and give me meat, and dress the meat in my sight, that I may see it, and eat it at her hand'" (II Samuel 13:1-5).

Amnon did exactly what Jonadab told him to do, and he told the king to have her make cakes for him in his sight. David then sent her to Amnon's house, and she found him lying in bed. She finally baked the cakes and put them before him, but he refused to eat. And he sent all the men out from him. He then said to Tamar to take the meat into his chamber, and she did as she was instructed. "And when she had brought them unto him to eat, he took hold of her, and said unto her, 'Come lie with me, my sister'. And she answered and said, 'Nay my brother, do not force me; for no such thing ought to be done in Israel: do not thou this folly'…but being stronger than she, forced her and lay with her" (vv.11-14). He became angry and exceedingly hated her and asked her to leave, but she refused. "Then he called his servant that ministered unto him, and said, 'Put now this woman out from me, and bolt the door after her'" (v.17). Wow! No matter what man does, God is still God!

Genesis of Different Tongues and Languages
(Ethnicity at the Tower of Babel)

The earth was repopulated by Noah's families after the flood. "These are the families of the sons of Noah, after their generations, in their nations: and by these were the nations divided in the earth after the flood" (Genesis 10:32). This is known as "The Table of Nations." It tells us that all the original nations of the world were formed from the descendants of Noah. The basis of this worldwide division was their dispersion at Babel.

"And the whole earth was of one language, and of one speech. And they said, 'Go to, let us build us a city and a tower, whose top may reach unto heaven; and let us make us a name, lest we be scattered abroad upon the face of the whole earth.' And the LORD came down to see the city and the tower, which the children of men builded. And the LORD said, 'Behold, the people is one, and they all have one language; and this they begin to do: and now nothing will be restrained from them, which they have imagined to do.' Go to, let us go down, and there confound their language, that they may not understand one another's language. So the LORD scattered them abroad…and they left off to build the city. Therefore, is the name of it called Babel; because the LORD did there confound the language of all the earth: and from thence did the LORD scatter them abroad upon the face of all the earth" (Genesis 11:1-9).

Is this the genesis of races? "One searches the Bible in vain for this information, for neither the word nor the concept of race appears in the Bible at all! There is no such thing as a race except for the human race! Skin color and other supposed racial characteristics are mere combinations of innate genetic factors, originally created in Adam and Eve to permit development of different family characteristics "as the human race was commanded to multiply and fill the earth" (Genesis 1:28, 9:1). "Race is strictly an evolutionary concept used by Darwin, Huxley, Haeckel, and other 19th century evolutionists to rationalize their white racism." But from the beginning, it was not so! "God that made the world and all things therein…hath made of one blood all nations of men for to dwell on all the face of the earth, and hath determined the times before appointed, and the bounds of their habitation" (Acts 17:24,26). Whenever I see the "Red Big Bus," I often wonder where they got the words "one blood." They did not get it from anywhere else except from the Bible! "Have we not all one father? hath not one God created us? why do we deal treacherously every man against his brother?" (Malachi 2:10)

Pride and boasting before God is vanity, and White supremacy is foolish. "Keep thy heart with all diligence; for out of it are the issues of life. Pride goeth before destruction, and an haughty spirit before a fall" (Proverbs 4:23, 16:18). Pride will never be tolerated in the presence of God. Our ancient foe was cast out of heaven because of pride! Their hearts were filled with pride at Babel and they decided to make a name for themselves by building a tower to reach unto heaven. This was the first tower ever built and known to man. They wanted to ascend to heaven like Satan. But the Lord came down and confounded their language and scattered them. This was something they never wanted to do. According to the New Testament version, "And hath made of one blood all nations of men (human race) for to dwell on all the face of the earth, and hath determined the times before appointed, and the bounds of their habitation" (Acts 17:26). (Isaiah 45:18). The continents of the world and their inhabitants, nations, languages, and ethnicity are the works of the Lord God!

Genesis of Family Feud: Siblings Rivalry, Jealousy, and Anger
Family feuds are common in every society. It is incredibly sad to see a family break up as they fight over inheritance, jealousy, hatred, or pride. This all started with Cain and Able in Genesis Chapter 4. We also read about a strife between Abram and Lot. "And there was a strife between the herdmen of Abram's cattle and the herdmen of Lot's cattle: and the Canaanite and the Perizzite dwelled then in the land. And Abram said unto Lot, 'Let there be no strife, I pray thee between me and thee, and between my herdmen and thy herdmen; for we be brethren. Is not the whole land before thee? Separate thy self, I pray thee from me: if thou wilt take the left hand, then I will go to the right; or if thou depart to the right hand, then I will go to the left'" (Genesis 13:7-9). Abraham showed great humility without selfish ambition and esteemed Lot better than himself. "Let nothing be done through strife or vain glory; but in lowliness of mind let each esteem other better than themselves...Let this mind be in you, which was also in Christ Jesus" (Philippians 2:3-5). Oh, how we desperately need such a mind today!

A classic case of this was between Abraham's wife Sarah and Hagar. "And Sarah saw the son of Hagar the Egyptian, which she had born unto Abraham, mocking. Wherefore she said unto Abraham, 'Cast out this bondwoman and her son: for the son of this bondwoman shall not be heir with my son, even with Isaac.' And God said unto Abraham, 'Let it not be grievous in thy sight because of the lad, and because of thy bondwoman; in all that Sarah hath said unto thee, hearken unto her voice; for in Isaac shall thy seed be called. And also of the son of the bondwoman will I make a nation, because he is thy seed'" (Genesis 21: 9-13). Adam did not say no to Eve when she gave him the fruit to eat, and Abraham did not say no to his wife Sarah when she told him to go unto Hagar. "And Sarai said unto Abram, 'Behold now, the LORD hath restrained me from bearing: I pray thee, go unto my maid; it may be that I may obtain children by her'. And Abram hearkened to the voice of Sarai" (Genesis 16:2).

The Bible has given us everything we need to know in life about patience, obedience, humility, love, peace, self-sacrifice, self-control, and much more. Yet we always fall short of living without reproach. Is it not the result of sin? There was feuding within Laban's family, too. "And Laban had two daughters: the name of the elder was Leah, and the name of the younger was Rachel. Leah was tender eyed; but Rachel was beautiful and well favoured" (Genesis 29:16-17). Jacob loved Rachel and was willing to serve Laban for seven years to marry her (v.18). He did serve Laban for the seven years, but he was deceived.

Jacob completed the seven years and asked Laban to give him Rachel. Laban held a feast in the evening and gave Leah to Jacob instead of Rachel. Jacob realized in the morning that he went unto Leah and not Rachel. "And it came to pass in the morning, behold, it was Leah: and he said to Laban, 'What is this thou hast done unto me? Did not I serve with thee for Rachel?' Wherefore then hast thou beguiled me?'" (v.25). Jacob was told that it was not customary for the younger to marry before the elder. Therefore, he agreed to serve another seven years to marry Rachel because he loved Rachel more than Leah (v.30).

Listen to God's sovereignty, "And when the Lord saw that Leah was hated, he opened her womb: but Rachel was barren" (v.31). Leah conceived and bare a son and called him Reuben and said, "Surely the LORD hath looked upon my affliction; now therefore my husband will love me" (v.32). Rachel became angry with her sister because she had no children. "Rachel envied her sister; and said unto Jacob, 'Give me children, or else I die.' And Jacob's anger was kindled against Rachel: and said, 'Am I in God's stead, who had withheld from thee the fruit of the womb?'" (Genesis 30:1-2).

The feud between the wives of Elkanah, Hannah, and Peninnah is another interesting one. The Bible said, "Peninnah had children, but Hannah had no children" (I Samuel 1:2). Elkanah made a yearly sacrifice unto the LORD of hosts in Shiloh (v. 3). "And when the time was that Elkanah offered, he gave to Peninnah his wife and to all her sons and her daughters, portions. But unto Hannah he gave a worthy portion; for he loved Hannah: but the Lord had shut her womb. And her adversary also provoked her sore, for to make her fret, because the Lord had shut her womb" (vv.4-6).

Year after year, Peninnah continued to provoked Hannah and she "wept and did not eat." Elkanah said to her, "Hannah, why weepest thou? And why eatest thou not and why is thy heart grieved? am not I better to thee than ten sons? (v.8). Hannah was bitter and poured her heart to the Lord to give her a son. Her husband thought she was drunk because she was not moving her lips. She made a vow unto the Lord that she will give the son to serve the Lord in the temple. The Lord eventually opened her womb, and she bare a son, and called his name Samuel, saying, Because I have asked him of the LORD (v.20).

Genesis of Slavery and Hatred in the Human Heart
As it is clearly shown in the book of Genesis, the depraved heart of humanity is unspeakable. The Bible only knows one race, and that is the human race. Thank God, only the Bible tells it like it is! American has yet to tell all of the truth about mob violence, lynching during slavery, and the Jim Crow Era. "The concept of race was created as a classification of human beings with the purpose of giving power to white people and to legitimize the dominance of white people over non-white people." Cain killed his brother because of anger that led to hatred and not racism! Joseph's brothers sold him to the Ish-mee-lites because of hatred and not racism. It then continued and has now become a pandemic. "The thoughts of our hearts will inevitably control the words on our lips and works of our hands."

Excluding one party to participate in a democratic process is not a true democracy. "But those things which proceed out of the mouth come forth from the heart; and they defile the man. For out of the heart proceed evil thoughts, murders, adulteries, thefts, false witness, blasphemies" (Matthew 15:18-19). The above two atrocities took place because of depravity of the mind. Pulse Massacre in Orlando, the Ocoee Massacre, and the Tulsa Massacre a two-day rampage in thriving black community known as "Black Wall Street" was completely burned to the ground.

These and any other massacres or atrocities in the world happened because of hatred, depravity of the mind, and "love of darkness rather than light because their deeds were evil" (John 3:19). All white people are blind and so are all black people. All white people are hypocrites and so are all black people! As a matter of fact, the whole human race is blind and are hypocrites. "Let them alone, they be blind leaders of the blind. And if the blind lead the blind, both shall fall into a ditch" (Matthew 15:14). "Thou hypocrite! First cast out the beam out of thine own eye; and then shalt thou see clearly to cast out the mote out of thy brother's eye" (Matthew 7:5). This is God's assessment of who we are, and who is going to claim supremacy in this? If I were to write the names of all blacks that were murdered in the hands of other blacks because of drugs, gangs, and gun violence, there would not be enough space to do that.

And if I were to write the names of all blacks who were lynched, died because of mob violence, and died in the hands of police, there would not be enough space to do that either. Therefore, it is time to call a spade a spade! There are a lot of unpleasant, shameful, unspeakable, and embarrassing issues in both black and white communities. Therefore, it is time, especially for blacks, to examine themselves and focus their eyes on the Lord Jesus Christ our Savior, not on politicians, trends, celebrities, and the pursuit of worldly material things that do not satisfy. "Incline my heart unto thy testimonies, and not to covetousness" (Psalm 119:36).

If your pastor is black or white and preaches not the wholesome word of God, he has perverted the gospel. "But though we, or an angel from heaven preach any other gospel unto you than that which we have preached unto you, let him be accursed" (Galatians 1:8). This is so serious that Paul repeats it in verse 9. American democracy and capitalism have proven not to be sufficient in being independent from the God of the Bible! Therefore, let us go to God because the whole human race cannot clean up themselves. "Come now and let us reason together, saith the LORD, though your sins be as scarlet, they shall be as white as snow; though they be red like crimson, they shall be as wool" (Isaiah 1:18). "Wherewithal shall a young man cleanse his way? By taking heed thereto according to thy word" (Psalms 119:9).

Divine revelation tells us that what we think we have in a democratic society has come up short. Blacks don't have to look up to white people because they claim to be superior. We have the Word of God, which is able to make us wise, cleanse our ways, and learn to be content. There are some white people who believe in Darwinian evolutionary philosophy and humanism. And if we continue to look up to them, and not to the Lord Jesus Christ, we will all fall into a ditch, which will cause us to be angry, hateful, and resentful. Since the fall of Adam in the Garden of Eden, the heart and spirit of man has been corrupted, whereby man is no longer in his rightful mind and can no longer walk in the ways of God! "Their feet run to evil, and they make haste to shed innocent blood: their thoughts are thoughts of iniquity; wasting and destruction are in their paths, there is no fear of God before their eyes" (Isaiah 59:7, Proverbs 1:16, Romans 3:15-18) This is what God said we are! Who can argue with God in this?

Look at what is going on around the world. Do you see the fear of God before the eyes of mankind? Is this not what happened in Ocoee, Tulsa, and in many other places in the world? These are all the works of darkness. Joseph was the most beloved of his father. "Now Israel loved Joseph more than all his children, because he was the son of his old age: and he made him a coat of many colours. And when his brethren saw that their father loved him more than all his brethren, they hated him more, and could not speak peaceably unto him" (Genesis 37:3-4). At this point on, the hatred and depravity of the heart were intensified. Joseph had a dream while they were working in the field.

The dream had to do with authority over his brethren and he told them about the dream. Listen to what they said, "Shalt thou have indeed reign over us? or shalt thou indeed have dominion over us? And they hated him yet more for his dreams, and for his words" (vv.7-8). He had another dream and told it to his brethren and his father. When the father was told about the dream, he rebuked Joseph. He said, "What is this dream that thou hast dreamed? Shall I and thy mother and thy brethren indeed come to bow down ourselves to thee to the earth?" (vv. 9-11). His father sent him to his brethren in the field, but he could not find them right away. He finally found them in Dothan. "And when they saw him afar off, even before he came near unto them, they conspired against him to slay him" (v.18). When he finally came to them, they stripped him of his coat of many colours and cast him into a pit and sat down to eat bread. As they were eating, they saw a company of Ish-mee-lites with camels and spices. "And Judah said unto his brethren, What profit is it if we slay our brother, and conceal his blood? Come let us sell him to the Ish-mee-lities, and let not our hand be upon him; for he is our brother and our flesh. And his brethren were content" (vv.23-27).

God's divine plan can never be derailed. Joseph later became a leader in his master's house in Egypt, which fulfilled his dreams (Genesis 45-50). There was some form of slavery in Africa before the Trans-Atlantic Slave Trade. There were tribal conflicts, and those that were captured during the conflicts were sold to other tribes to be servants. This practice became prominent and well-established during the British and French Colonial Eras. The slave business became very profitable, and many powerful people depended on it so much that a publicist for the West Indies Trade wrote, "The impossibility of doing without slaves in the West Indies will always prevent traffic being dropped. The necessity, the absolute necessity, then of carrying it on must since there is no other, be its excuse." Slavery was referred to by some as "Black Gold" because slavery built the wealth of many European countries. Is slavery a good thing? No, but God can use any evil situation to bring glory and honor to himself! He had declared that His thoughts and His ways are different from ours (Isaiah 55:8-9). Unfortunately, those that were captured in tribal conflicts were sold to the British and the French, and it was later legitimized and became a very lucrative business, as indicated by the West Indies Trade. This became an easy way to make a living without the sweat of their faces. There were African chiefs in the south-eastern part of Nigeria, especially in the Delta Region and parts of Ibo land, that were involved in this unspeakable trade. Ghana was the main shipping port and had the Elmina Castle with its door of no return. The Elmina Castle is still standing today!

Jerry Rawlings, who was the President of Ghana in 1994, apologized for the African role in slavery. They all have evil hearts and depraved minds with seared consciences. The Pathfinder, David Livingstone, witnessed unspeakable atrocities and brutality of the slaves by Arab slave traders in Africa. I watched documentaries on PBS about mob lynching of blacks and other atrocities that are still too painful for me to comprehend. Human beings were sold as livestock in a slave market. In 1838, Georgetown University sold 272 slaves to keep the university afloat. Virginia Theological Seminary (VTS), "For all its prominence, depended for decades on the labor of Black people who were never paid adequately for their labor or were never paid at all." Wow! A Theological Seminary? If this is not racism, what is? This is pure evil and manifestation of a depraved mind too! This injustice and feeling of white supremacy took place from 1823 to 1951. Why did this evil continue for over a century? Bob Jones University was founded in 1927, and in 2000 they acknowledged that they had failed too.

"And let everyone that nameth the name of Christ depart from iniquity" (II Timothy 2:19). VTS has started to make amends, reconciliations, and reparations in the form of cash to known descendants of those slaves. The Southern Baptist Convention was founded in 1845, and in 1995, it had a resolution on racial reconciliation. They finally recognized that their relationship with African Americans had been hindered right from its inception, and the role slavery played and the fact that many of their forebears defended the right to own slaves. Why did it take a century and a half for them to make amends?

Calvary Baptist Church in New York City was founded in 1847, and in 1961 there was a turning point! Again, why did it take over a century to witness a turning point? "For as long as anyone could remember, Calvary had barred Black Americans from membership. The anomaly of racial bias was out of sync with the word of God. Additions to our church must ever be controlled by the saving and sovereign work of the Holy Spirit and not governed by racial prejudice or discrimination. A congregation must consist of a society of saved sinners, irrespective of color or class distinction. Anything less than this is alien to the New Testament principles concerning a local fellowship," shares Dr. Stephen Olford, former Senior Pastor from 1959-1973.

I believe it is time for all white congregations to step out and bridge the gap and acknowledge their sins of the past. People that have named the name of Christ tolerated segregation and white supremacy for centuries. If white supremacy is not systematic, why did segregation go on for centuries, pastor after pastor, in white congregations? If people with defiled minds outside the church are doing it, the church ought not to have followed them. The saints of the past, such as David Livingstone, C.T. Studd, George Grenfell, Hudson Taylor, Mary Slessor, and Amy Carmichael left a great legacy for us all to follow, especially to White evangelicals.

"Wherefore come out from among them, and be ye separate, saith the Lord, and touch not the unclean thing; and I will receive you" (2 Corinthians 6:17). In 1908, colored Methodist Bishops appealed to white Americans to assist for the removal of Jim Crow Laws. But the appeal fell on deaf ears! Please note, I am not trying to teach children to be hateful or to make young adults or older adults feel guilty or uncomfortable in something that their forebears did. In 1963, George Wallace, the former governor of Alabama, declared, "segregation now, segregation tomorrow, segregation forever." Integration in our congregations now, integration in our congregations tomorrow, and integration in our congregations forever. Was this the response from white evangelicals? Please note, I am not trying to open a can of worms.

Do we really hold these truths to be self-evident that all men are created equal? It is one thing to have something on a piece of paper and another thing to truly carry it out to express its meaning socially, politically, and economically. Thank God no one can claim superiority at the foot of the Cross! Lynching of Native Americans and Japanese Internment Camps completely negate these truths. As an expatriate observer, I don't think it is time for America, especially white congregations, to look in the rear-view mirror and celebrate. Bloody Sunday led to a major victory in voting rights, but these rights are slowing being eaten away. Redistricting with its intentions to limit the rights of a group of people to exercise their constitutional right is not a true democracy. Remember! "A little leaven" (Galatians 5:9). Is this going to take us back slowly to the Jim Crow Era? There were demonstrations everywhere when George Floyd was murdered. Central Florida Public Radio (NPR) visited a white evangelical congregation. Please forgive me, I don't remember the city and the name of the church. Maybe someone would say, I only heard what I wanted to hear. This is far from the truth.

I was listening to hear truth that would indicate to me that they recognized the problem and were striving or have an on-going desire to be "salt and light" that the Bible calls us to be! I was listening to hear a Biblical solution such as, "Create in me [us] a clean heart, O God; and renew a right spirit within me [us]" (Psalm 51:10). "And be not conformed to this world: (any behavior that is contrary to Scriptures) but be ye transformed by the renewing of your mind, that ye may prove what is that good, and acceptable, and perfect, will of God" (Romans 12:2). "And have no fellowship with the unfruitful works of darkness, but rather reprove them" (Ephesians 5:11). The reporter asked the pastor about how members of the congregation see racism. The pastor said that whenever racism is mentioned, the temperature within the congregation drops to zero and there is complete silence, but when abortion is mentioned, the temperature rises and there is much enthusiasm! Please note, these are not direct quotes, but they speak to the vexing problems.

In my opinion, we have allowed politicians to use abortion to divide the church. How much do they care about the children born who have no health insurance? We don't need politicians who have "a form of godliness, but denying the power thereof" (2 Timothy 3:5). and who don't care about the gospel of Jesus Christ but simply use us to win elections. I believe that it is time for black and white congregations to focus their attentions on Christ and not on a political party or politicians who honor Christ with their lips but, their hearts are far from Him.

White supremacy, or whatever name you want to call it, has been going on for centuries because it is structured, well-ordered, and planned. Is redlining not structured, well-ordered, and planned? If it is not, why do we still have redlining and other forms of systematic racism today? I don't think that young people have to be taught to feel superior to non-whites, especially to black people. They see how the Native Americans and Asian Americans were treated and are still treated today. They already know it, they see it, they hear it, and they can smell it in every facet of American life. When a black child used a pool in a white community and the pool was later drained, what does this mean or say about blacks in general? "When mother-cow is chewing grass, its young ones watch its mouth."

When I was growing up, my people despised and belittled a different ethnic group. I was never taught to despise them, but I used the same derogatory language that is directed to that ethnic group. Do I do that anymore? Thank God I don't! In Nigeria, different tribes feel superior to other tribes and use derogatory language to show their superiority. Human beings are always proud and like to feel superior to others. Therefore, this kind of attitude toward others is not limited to a particular group of people, but it is a worldwide problem! The Bible said, "All have sinned and come short of the glory of God" (Romans 3:23). "Any natural man, no matter how powerful, is afflicted with the lethal disease of sin." It is true that the word "sin" makes some people uneasy. Could this be a reason why some preachers do not say anything about sin in preaching the everlasting gospel? If they don't, they have handled the Word of God deceitfully without "the power of God unto salvation" (Romans 1:16).

Therefore, I believe it is time, for white evangelicals especially, and for every Christian to look at themselves in the mirror and listen to this, "For the time is come that judgment must begin at the house of God: and if it first begin at us, what shall the end be of them that obey not the gospel of God?" (1 Peter 4:17) You see, it begins with us Christians and not with politicians, lawmakers, celebrities, and talk show hosts who perhaps only honor God with their lips, but their hearts are far from Him.

Christians ought to take the lead to bring about reconciliation. Today, white supremacy is still a problem in some white congregations and within society. It has caused great strife between blacks and whites. How long do we allow this to go on? Even though we know and have read that, "For there is no respect of persons with God" (Romans 2:11). How can we be the "salt and light" that the Bible says we are? He hath called us out of darkness into his marvelous light (I Peter 2:9). If Christ is the gamechanger, let us then live like that for the world to see that we are peculiar people. Is the world listening to us or seeing us as true disciples of Christ? The Lord said, "A new commandment I give unto you. That ye love one another; as I have loved you that ye also love one another. By this shall all men know that ye are my disciples if ye love one to another" (John 13:34-35). Today, most people know that Christians are divided as Congress.

Listen to this, "Though there is great antipathy in the human heart to the gospel of Christ, yet when Christians make their good work shine, all admire them. It is when great disparity exists between profession and practice that we secure the scorn of mankind." Yes, on the 6th of November 2012, the 3rd of November 2016, and the 8th of November 2020, the Church of Jesus Christ secured the scorn of mankind and showed the world how divided they really are! They exhibited behavior that was quite foolish and shameful. Those outside the church were shaking their heads. "Now I beseech you, brethren, by the name of our Lord Jesus Christ, that ye all speak the same thing, and that there be no divisions among you; but that ye be perfectly joined together in the same mind and in the same judgement" (I Corinthians 1:10).

It is true that Christians will never be perfect on this side of the grave. Christians are not robots, they have free will and can disagree with one another like any other group of people. A case in point, "Separation of Paul and Barnabas" (Acts 15:36-39).But we ought to have an on-going desire to bridge the gap between profession and practice. Christians ought not to take their cues from politicians, but from the infallible Word of God! It is sometimes shameful for me to read, "Live like Jesus did, and the world will listen. I like your Christ, I do not like your Christians. Your Christians are so unlike your Christ." This was a challenge from Mahatma Gandhi to us Christians.

Ancient Greece, the Roman Empire, Ancient Egypt, and every known civilization has been involved in slavery in one form or another. Slavery is as old as prostitution! We still have some forms of slavery today! Despite the advancements in technology and an increase standard of living, the heart of man is still deceitful above all things and desperately wicked from the time of Cain to the present. There is no form of government that can meet human's greatest need of salvation. America has always been proud of her democracy, rule of law, reliance on human wisdom, and strength. However, listen to this statement that cannot be denied, "Wherefore let him that thinketh he standeth take heed lest he fall" (I Corinthians 10:12). This is not just for individuals, but for families, congregations, nations, and organizations.

The 6th of January 2021 riots at the seat of American Democracy proved this point. Some Christian leaders and laymen that have put their trust, focus, and leaning on politicians were disappointed so much so that they believed lies about the 2020 election being stolen. Some also believe in the so-called "Pizza Gate" and other propagandas. What happened to discernment? How is it that Christians are so easily deceived? Today, the United States is grappling with unprecedented propagandas, lies, alternative truth which is not truth at all, police brutality, racism, and complacency of White Evangelical Congregations! If politicians and lawmakers refused to acknowledge and teach history like it is, the Bible says, "For this they willingly are ignorant" (2 Peter 3:5).

Christians don't need politicians and law makers; we can teach history in our congregations from a biblical perspective that in the sight of God, we are all lepers like Naaman the Syrian in II Kings 5! We have all been "weighed in the balances and found wanting" (Daniel 5:27). Silence does not heal wounds, but an on-going action or desire to do the right thing does. Repealing of established civil rights exacerbates the vexing problems in society. Is anyone wise enough to argue with God? The Bible does not have good things to say about mankind because we are vile, wicked, and evil. "Dark is the stain we cannot hide." Truth only stands on the Word of God. "No gift or genius or position can keep us safe from sin." Christians anywhere in the world are disciples of Christ and we do know the truth that He had made us alive in Christ and reconciled us to Himself. "Old things are passed away; behold all things are become new" (II Corinthians 5:17). So that we may live to glorify Him and Him alone!

"And ye shall know the truth, and the truth shall make you free. If the Son therefore shall make you free, ye shall be free indeed" (John 8:32, 36). Yes indeed, we are free because of Calvary and nothing else! Is there a group of people that can pull themselves up by their bootstraps? King David, the man after God's own heart, penned Psalm 51 after Nathan the prophet confronted him after he had gone into Bathsheba! There is no alibi in this Psalm, and it gives us a clear, step-by-step outline of what God requires, how to get right with God, and the result of genuine repentance. In my opinion, I believe this to be a Psalm for individuals, families, institutions, and nations. Yes indeed, it has the answer to the myriads of human dilemmas we face today. Why did God still put up with us for so long?

Genesis of Desperate Housewife and the Sovereignty of God

There is a popular American comedy TV drama called "Desperate Housewives." But before this drama, the Bible recorded a real Desperate Housewife, Portiphar's wife. Joseph's brother sold him into slavery to the Ish-mee-lites. But the Lord was with him and made him prosper. Even though he was a slave, he was faithful and served his master well and had a good testimony and glorified the Lord. "And his master saw that the LORD was with him, and that the LORD made all that he did to prosper in his hand" (Genesis 39:3). But by grace, he became the overseer in his master's house. "And Joseph found grace in his sight, and he served him: and he made him overseer over his house, and all that he had he put into his hand" (v. 4). "And Joseph was a goodly person and well favoured. And it came to pass after these things, that his master's wife cast her eyes upon Joseph; [lust of the eyes] and she said 'Lie with me.' But he refused and said unto his master's wife, 'Behold, my master wotteth not what is with me in the house, and he hath committed all that he hath to my hand; There is no greater in this house than I…because thou hath his wife: how then can I do this wickedness and sin against God?' And it came to pass, as she spake to Joseph day by day, that he hearkened not unto her, to lie by her or to be with her. And it came to pass about this time, that Joseph went into the house… there was none of the men of the house there within. And she caught him by his garment, saying, 'Lie with me:' and he left his garment in her hand, and fled, and got him out. That she called unto the men of her house, and spake to them, saying, 'See, he hath brought in an Hebrew unto us to mock us; he came in unto me to lie with me, and I cried with a loud voice…that he left his garment with me, and fled, and got him out.' And she laid up his garment by her, until his lord came home" (vv.4-16). She lied to her husband about what she said he did to her and he believed her, and Joseph was thrown into prison.

"But the Lord was with Joseph, and showed him mercy, and gave him favour in the sight of the keeper of the prison. And the keeper of the prison committed to Joseph's hand all the prisoners that were in the prison; and whatsoever they did there, he was the doer of it. The keeper of the prison looked not to anything that was under his hand; because the LORD was with him, and that which he did, the Lord made it to prosper" (vv.21-23). Here the Lord had left the curtain ajar for us to see His sovereignty. God used Joseph to interpret Pharaoh's dream, and Joseph became the second in command in Egypt (Genesis (41:40-41). There was great famine in Canaan and Joseph's father Jacob sent his children to Egypt to buy corn. They had no clue that their brother Joseph was the man in charge of the sale of the corn. He knew who they were, but they did not know who he was.

And he never revealed himself to them. In the fullness of time, he finally revealed himself and kept them at ease. "And he said, I am Joseph your brother, whom ye sold into Egypt. Now therefore be not grieved, nor angry with yourself, that ye sold me hither: for God did send me before you to preserve life" (Genesis 45:4-5). God finally opened the curtain wide. Their father had died, and they were afraid and thought that Joseph will repay evil for evil. "And they sent a messenger unto Joseph, saying, 'Thy father did command before he died, saying, So shall ye say unto Joseph, Forgive, I pray thee now, the trespass of thy brethren, and their sin; for they did unto thee evil…'And Joseph wept when they spake unto him. And his brethren also went and fell down before his face…Behold, we be thy servants. Joseph's dreams had come true, perhaps they said to themselves he told us!" (Genesis 37:7-9) Then Joseph said unto them, "Fear not: for am I in the place of God? But as for you, ye thought evil against me; but God meant it unto good, to bring to pass, as it is this day, to save much people alive" (Genesis 50:16-20). Joseph had no intention to repay his brothers with evil.

Skeptics, please take note, there is no Stockholm Syndrome in this! The life of Joseph was very remarkable and was all about the sovereignty of God. God's involvement was not clearly seen in the beginning of Joseph's life. Through all that happened to him, "Joseph remains faithful in the dark days. Joseph remains useful in the dark days and Joseph remains hopeful in the dark days." Amen and Amen!

Conclusion

I believe that the most important debate in the history of mankind is creationism versus evolutionism. God clearly gives mankind His account of everything that He created in the Book of Genesis. A person's philosophical view of the world and of God will fall into either "creation" or "evolution." According to evolutionist Carl Sagan, the universe is "eternal." Darwin's Survival of the Fittest is nothing but a culture of death. As per Steve Jobs, "death clears out the old to make way for the new." There are so many sufferings in the world, and evolutionists cannot show the "root cause of societal ills." However, the Bible declares that the universe and all of its creatures were created by God, and only the Bible clearly and truly identifies the root cause of societal ills as sin.

I know, the word sin makes some people uneasy. "If there had been no sin, there would have been no suffering." And sin has caused us to be separated from God, and we are no longer in our "rightful mind" and have instead become vain in our imaginations. Richard Dawkins, author of *The God Delusion*, is also an evolutionary scientist. "The GOD Delusion makes a compelling case that belief in God is not just wrong but potentially deadly." How? This is what the Bible called "vain imaginations" (Romans 1:21). In all of his studies, research, observations, and writings, Dawkins was unable to pinpoint the root cause of suffering and problems within mankind. Which is more deadly? Believe in Evolution, Survival of the Fittest, Natural Selection, or Creation? Well, if you don't believe in God, you will believe in the illicit drug delusion, gangs, and gun violence, which are far more compelling with undisputable proofs than "The God Delusion." In 2018, "a total of 67,367 drug overdose deaths occurred in the United

States, a 4.1% decline from 2017; 46,802 (69.5%) involved an opioid." The Center for Health Statistics (HCHS) drug overdose deaths release covered a one-year period from 2018 and ending in February 2019. An estimated 69,029 people died of overdose. "Nearly 7 out of 10 of these overdose deaths were due to opioids. Alcohol related deaths increased between 2019 and 2020 from 78,927 deaths to 99,017. The number of opioids overdose deaths increased 38% in 2020, with a 55% increase in deaths involving synthetic opioids such as fentanyl. The U.S. has the highest overdose rates from all three leading drugs; Opioids, Amphetamine, and Cocaine."

I think this could cause the nation to cry out, "Woe is us." This is the consequence of belief in "Illicit Drug Delusion." How many people in the same period died who believed in God, except for natural causes? Does the U.S. consider these many deaths acceptable? Is the U.S. winning the war on drugs? "In ascribing the power to choose to unintelligent natural forces, Darwin perpetuated the greatest intellectual swindle in the history of ideas. Nature has no power to choose." Randy Guliuzza is a Biblical Creationist, a brilliant M.D., a Professional Engineer and the President of Institute for Creation Research (ICR). As a professional engineer, he applied the root cause analysis, which shows the legacy of pain and all sorts of immorality ever known to man! Therefore, in order to correctly diagnose societal ills, the root cause analysis approach is of paramount importance. There are myriads of programs attempting to solve so many of the problems that plague us. Billions of dollars have been spent on illicit drugs consumption and billions of dollars have been spent on drug treatments and gun violence programs.

Listen to this, "Wherefore do ye spend money for that which is not bread? and your labour for that which satisfieth not? hearken diligently unto me, and eat ye that which is good, and let your soul delight itself in fatness" (Isaiah 55:2). To make America great again, America must turn back to the Bible! I thank God for all the treatment programs, and the progress that they have made are commendable. However, evolutionists who do not believe in divine revelation are unable to find the root cause of societal ills. Creationists who believe in divine revelation use the root cause analysis. Therefore, is it the evolutionists or creationists that are treating symptoms and wasting valuable time? There is still strife among the disciples of Christ in local congregations. The Christians are the ones to bring about reconciliation, not the politicians!

Author's Note

I was born in Nigeria from the Ijaw Tribe in the Delta Region. The motto of my elementary school inspired me to be an observer in the United States. It reads: "The End Crowns the Work." It reads in Latin "Finis Coronat Opus." This quote was traditionally attributed to the Roman poet Ovid. The Biblical reference for this motto is found in the Gospel according to Saint Luke, 14:28-30. I never gave thought to the meaning of this statement and the three stanzas of the old Nigerian National Anthem, until I have been in the United States. The anthem was composed by a British expatriate, Lillian Jean Williams. This anthem was in use from 1960-1978. The first stanza reads:

"Nigeria we hail thee,
Our own dear native land,
Though tribe and tongue may differ,
In brotherhood we stand…"

This became an awakening for me in the United States, and I started giving thoughts to words and their meanings. The most important debate I witnessed in secondary school was "A Pen is Mightier Than a Sword." In the United States, I read articles by evolutionists and creationists, listened to talk shows and debates between evolutionists and creationists, and watched documentaries and talk shows about the myriads of societal ills on television. This was the first time I developed a keen interest in observing Western intellectual thoughts on ethics, morality, philosophy, religion, and science.

It was also the first time, I was exposed to wholesome words and sound biblical doctrines at Calvary Baptist Church in New York City with clarity, and I believed the Holy Bible, the Word of God, as the absolute moral standard. At the end of a talk show or a debate, I would always ask myself, "What is the takeaway in what I have just witnessed or observed? Was there an ultimate standard applied to analyze the root cause of societal ills?"

The think tanks like The Aspin Institute, The Brookings Institution, The Cato Institute, The Heritage Foundation, Center for American Progress, the Democrats, and the Republicans cannot solve the myriads of societal ills that have plagued America and the rest of humanity for centuries. But glory be to God, at the end of a talk show or a TV documentary, I no longer ask "What is the takeaway?" because of the Word of God, the Holy Bible, now holds my conscience captive. And as per Christian apologist and philosopher Francis Schaeffer, "If there is no absolute moral standard, then one cannot say in a final sense that anything is right or wrong, By absolute we mean that which always applies, that which provides a final or ultimate standard. There must be an absolute if there are to be morals, and there must be an absolute if there are to be values. If there is no absolute beyond man's ideas, then there is no final appeal to judge between individuals and groups whose moral judgements conflict. We are merely left with conflicting opinions." Amen and Amen!

Therefore, I can boldly keep my integrity, reputation, and conversation [manner of life] under the demands of Scriptures. Therefore, my elementary school motto, the old Nigerian National Anthem, debates of any kind, ethics, morality, philosophy, science, and religion are enlightened by the Word of God, and I no longer leave with conflicting opinions. The United States and every other nation are in a perpetual struggle to acknowledge the written word of God, the Holy Bible, as the absolute moral standard. Listen to this; "Ever learning, and never able to come to the knowledge of the truth" (II Timothy 3:7). The Holy Bible is the only gamechanger in everything. Therefore, it is either the Word of God or Homo-mensura "Man is the measure of all things."

Is America living in an era of alternative truth and the end justifies the means for political convenience? Is the church ordained by God the primary agent to accomplish His work on earth or the political parties or talk show hosts? The consequences of sin are clearly seen every day in the world and in the lives of people. Is humanity ready to believe the God of the Bible? To effectively tackle a problem, one must know what caused it. A doctor must correctly diagnose a disease to help the sick person get better. If a building collapses, engineers will use root cause analysis to probe with ever-deepening questions about what triggered the accident. Unless the true cause is identified, a professional problem solver is left either treating symptoms or wasting valuable time.

A similar approach could be taken with societal ills. What is the cause of so many of the problems that plague us? The Bible calls the root cause sin, and "sin had left a crimson stain" on everything. "Wherefore, as by one man sin entered into the world, and death by sin, and so death passed upon all men, for that all have sinned" (Romans 5:12). Sin has separated us from God as it separated Adam and Eve from God. Listen to this wonderful statement, "But God commendeth his love toward us, in that, while we were yet sinners, Christ died for us" (v. 8). "For as in Adam all die, [the bad news] even so in Christ shall all be made alive" [the good news] (I Corinthians 15:22). Amen and Amen!

References

Carl Sagan, *Cosmos,* Random House Publishing Group: New York, 1983.

Hannah Ritchie and Max Roser, "Opioids, Cocaine, Cannabis & Illicit Drugs," *Our World in Data,* December 2019.

Henry Morris III, "Three Worldly Powers," *Days of Praise,* September 16, 2018.

Henry Morris III, "Satan's Strategic Plan," *Days of Praise,* October 28, 2018.

Henry Morris, "Creation and the New Year," *Days of Praise,* 1 January 2020.

Henry Morris, "The Flesh and the Spirit," *Days of Praise,* 25 April 2020.

Henry Morris, "Origin of the Races," *Days of Praise,* 21 December 2020.

Henry Morris, "We are His Image," *Days of Praise,* 26 October 2019.

John Morris, "Clothing," *Days of Praise,* 11 October 2019.

John Morris, "The Man Born Blind," *Days of Praise,* 11 October 2019.

Randy Guliuzza, "Evolution Maligns Christian Edification," *Acts & Facts,* November 2019.

Randy Guliuzza, "Survival of the Fittest and Evolution's Death Culture," *Acts & Facts,* January 2020.

Richard Dawkins, *The God Delusion,* New York: Bantam Books, 2006.

The Holy Bible: King James Version, World Bible Publishers Iowa Falls, Iowa.

58